THE SPIRIT IS SKATING

THE SPIRIT IS SKATING

Charleston, SC
www.PalmettoPublishing.com

The Spirit is Skating
Copyright © 2022 by Roberta Walker Steverson

First Edition

Hardcover: 979-8-88590-540-4
Paperback: 979-8-88590-541-1

The Spirit is SKATING

BY: ROBERTA WALKER STEVERSON

This Book Is Dedicated to the following:

Sandra Anna Steverson Brannigan,
one of the seven angels that God
blessed me to mother.

&

The memory of 10 Black people
who were killed at Tops Market in Buffalo,
New York on May 14, 2022

&

The memory of 19 students and 2 teachers
killed at Robb Elementary School in Uvalde,
Texas on May 27, 2022

Sandra's mother and father had cautioned her again and again that she was a Black girl, and little Black girls could not do all of the things that little White girls could do, especially in this small, white, western New York college community of Brockport, New York, where they lived.

Hadn't her father said many times, "Sandra, the white man will grin in your face and then stab you in the back?"

And her mother had added, "Don't ever trust white people, Sandra. They will pretend to be your friends, but deep down, they think and always will think they are better than you." Her parents had spoken from experience, but all of their warnings, all of their prejudices, had fallen on innocently deaf ears.

Sandra was a regular at the all-white, Catholic, school she had attended since kindergarten. Oh sure, she had had a few racial remarks flung at her, but only two had bothered her—and those only momentarily, for now they were forgotten- Last year a fifth-grade boy had called her a nigger when she sat beside him on the shuttle bus, but she had told the principal, Sister Catherine, and he had been reprimanded. Likewise, in first grade her "good friend" Kim had called her Blacky, but Kim had said she was sorry at lunchtime after discovering that Sandra had an extra gingerbread cookie. Thus, Sandra had given Kim the extra cookie.

Unlike her mother, Sandra had been invited to all of the birthday parties and all of the pajama parties—that is, all but one. Last August, one of her good friends, Patty Gallo, had cried like a baby as she sobbed to Sandra in total bewilderment that her mother would not let Patty invite Sandra to her sleepover, birthday party. Patty could invite all of the other young ladies in her class, but not Sandra. The girls could not begin to understand why Mrs. Gallo was being so mean and hateful? Thus, they chose to dismiss the whole thing as "quirky adult stuff" and refused to let it interfere with their friendship. Excluding Patty, Sandra had been to her other friends' homes numerous times, and they, in turn, had been to hers. She just couldn't understand what it was her parents were talking about. The fifth-grade boy and Kim called everybody names. And Patty had wanted so much to invite Sandra to her party. Why all these warnings? Why all the fuss about color?

Sandra was not a typical Black. She was a typical fifth-generation "Oreo," a name that an obscure line of Blacks called themselves because they were black on the outside and impregnated with white people's attitudes and ideas on the inside. These Oreos were descendants of mixed Blacks, Native Americans, and Whites families who, after the Civil War, left the South and settled in rural areas around Rochester and Buffalo, New York. They usually married other Oreos and gradually grew and spread out all over the western part of New York State.

Sandra's family was even more obscure than other Oreos in that they were Catholic rather than the traditional Southern Baptist, and also, because they had a great deal of Native American blood mixed up in them. This accounted for Sandra's long, silky black hair, which had only a gentle touch of the customary tight, black curls throughout it. Her skin was beautiful. The coloring matched the soft brown of a baby deer. Her lips were not full. They were not thin. They were just perfect, and her almond-shaped eyes sparkled like two ebony marbles.

The most painful lesson Oreo and other Black children learned was that they were accepted only so far by their white friends and neighbors. Hadn't it been that way for Sandra's mother, Roberta? She had been raised from age five to a teenager in Scottsville, New York, during the late forties and mid-fifties. Mingle in school, sometimes! Too often during lunch hour , Roberta could be found hiding out in the girl's restroom because she had no one to play with. Mingle after school, no! Roberta had not been invited to any of her "friends'" birthday or pajama parties. The same had held true for Sandra's father, Lewis, who had been raised in LeRoy, New York, during the same period. Following his marriage, Lewis had been unsuccessful in renting an apartment, a house, or even a shack from people he had known all his life. Some he had played with in pre-school. Others had been his classmates in LeRoy's elementary, middle, and high school. But as Mr. Steverson's "friends" grew up they rejected him and his family. Socializing with Blacks was frowned upon, and renting to Blacks decreased the value of your property.

Ten years before Sandra was born, Mr. Steverson had passed the rigid test and met the demanding qualifications to become one of the first Blacks on a previously all-white New York State Police force. He was still battling negative, racist attitudes in and out of the division. Black was not the acceptable color for becoming a member of this "good-ole-boys'" club.

Her three older, grown sisters, Noni, Angi, and Janet, had experienced some of the same problems as their parents, but they had been treated a little better. They had been invited to a few parties. Yet hadn't her sister Janet longingly hoped to be asked to the senior prom? No White boy from Brockport, New York, in 1980, would dare to ask a Black girl to the high school prom. His reputation was at stake. Ironically, the White girls drooled over her sixteen-year-old brother, Lewis Anthony. They would go anywhere with Anthony, if only he would ask them. Her two preschool sisters, Michelle Maria and Anna-Maria Alana, well, they were like Sandra, their world was perfect, wasn't it?

For weeks, Sandra had been dreaming about and looking forward to the annual fourth-grade roller-skating party at Nativity of the Blessed Virgin Mary School which she attended. Throughout the regular school day, she and her two best friends, Kim and Madeline, had been conversing over this activity. Kim had been asked by five boys to skate with her in one of the three sweetheart rounds. Madeline had been asked by six boys, and the same number had asked Sandra. Kim was a bit upset at having had fewer boys ask her than had asked her friends, but she didn't let her jealousy show.

The girls giggled as the last bell rang. Quickly, they stuffed their books into their already cramped desks and scurried down the steps to the basement gym, which had been converted by the Roller Palace men into a temporary skating rink. Everything was ready for the children to have a good time. On the west wall, directly across from the entrance to the gym, was a record player. The youngsters would skate to music. In the middle of the floor, after having assured Sister Catherine that it would clean up spotless, the men had painted a large white oval. Seven feet away, on the outside of the first oval, they'd painted another. This would be the strip where the children would skate. Rows and rows of pink and blue streamers hung along the wall near the ovals. Attached to the streamers were dozens of pink and blue balloons, and along the back of the north and south walls, thirty-five chairs were lined up, seventeen on one side and eighteen on the other. The children would rest here in between rounds of skating. High above the chairs, high above the record player, and high enough to be seen in every corner of the room was a large wooden crucifix, which went unnoticed now by the boys and girls as they hurried into their rented skates. The children would have nine rounds of skating; six single rounds where they skated alone and three sweetheart rounds where they skated with a partner. The pattern being first two single rounds, and then one double. And they would follow this pattern until all the rounds of skating had been completed.

As the music started for the first round, Sandra eagerly finished tying her skates. Her slender legs wobbled as she rose from the chair. Maybe it was from inexperience? Maybe it was from excitement?

8

But it certainly was not from apprehension. This was going to be a great day!

Very carefully, Sandra maneuvered over to her two friends, who were impatiently waiting on the edge of the strip for her. Madeline reached out and caught Sandra's left hand, and then Sandra took hold of Kim's left hand. The three friends supported each other as they joined their classmates on the strip. The girls were lively! The music was bouncy! The whole room was swirling and moving—that is, everything except the crucifix. It was standing still....................

The girls laughed and giggled as they skated behind two boys, Peter and Paul. "Look how slow Peter is skating," Sandra said to her friends. "It looks like this is the first time he's ever been on roller skates."

"It probably is," Madeline said. "He can't get much of a chance to skate out on the farm."

"That's right," Kim added. "There aren't any sidewalks to skate on out there."

The trio waved and shouted to the boys as they shot past them. They were picking up speed when suddenly Kim cried out, "Stop pulling me, Madeline. You're going to make me fall." Madeline and Sandra paid no attention to Kim's admonition, and just as she started to cry out for the second time, they came to a sharp turn in the strip, and Kim fell helplessly to the floor.

"I told you to stop pulling me," Kim screamed at Madeline. "Look what you did to my knee."

"Oh, Kim," Sandra piped in, "I thought you said you were such a good skater?"

"I am," Kim pouted and turned her tear-filled eyes away from her classmates who were whirling by. "But it's awful hard to keep your balance when people are pulling you."

"We weren't pulling you." Madeline said defensively. "In fact, we were holding you up."

"That's not true!" Kim whined, putting her hands on her hips. "I can skate better than both of you." Then, rising slowly from the floor, favoring her bruised knee, Kim turned sharply away from Sandra and Madeline and rolled slowly over to a row of chairs.

"What a bad sport," Madeline said to Sandra as they gracefully rotated their position to once again challenge the strip.

"Yeah!" replied Sandra, shaking her pretty head in agreement. "She sure is a bad sport."

The two friends continued skating. The afflictions of their pouting friend became less and less significant to them as they yielded to the magic of the room, calling out to and joking with the other skaters. When the music ended, Sandra and Madeline began to feel a little guilty over the fact that they were having so much fun and Kim was just sitting in the chair biting her nails and rubbing her bruised knee. Thus, they delicately approached her and asked if she wanted to skate with them in the second round. Kim stopped rubbing her knee long enough to glare at them through her crystal-clear blue eyes and answered,

"No thanks! My knee is killing me."

Still glaring, she tossed her pretty, red hair away from her face and held her head in a queenly manner, adding,

"I'm waiting for the first sweetheart round. Peter asked me to skate that one with him, and I know he will be gentle. He has never pulled me or made me fall."

This remark caught Sandra by surprise. Yesterday, Peter had asked her to skate this particular round with him. Jerking her head around to face Kim, she insisted,

"Peter couldn't have asked you to skate this round with him, Kim. He told me yesterday that he was saving that one especially to skate with me."

"Well, he sure can't skate with both of you at the same time," Madeline remarked.

"He sure can't," Kim chanted. Then, wanting a little revenge for her tribulations, Kim smirked at Sandra with a "big-wide -grin" on her face, saying,

" He certainly wouldn't choose to skate with a Black girl when he can skate with a White girl."

Sandra cringed and shuddered at Kim's unexpected, hateful, and offensive words. She felt like she had been kicked in the stomach! It was a hard blow! It was the biggest betrayal Sandra had ever suffered. For the first time in her young life, Sandra became aware of the color difference between her and her friends. She could not respond to the remark because she had never prepared herself for the possibility of its existence. This was the grinning and the stabbing of which her father had spoken of. The stabbing wouldn't have hurt so much if the grinning hadn't preceded it.

Sandra was hurt! She was hurt badly! But she tried not to let it show as she quietly turned away from her friends. In a daze, she returned to the strip, where everyone except Kim had begun their second round. Sandra's heart was motionless, but the inner force of determination made her feet follow the white paint and direct her skates around the strip.

Slowly, Sandra's hurt turned to anger. Unable to hold her feelings inside any longer, she looked over at Madeline, who had inched in beside her, and said,

"Kim thinks she's so smart. She's so darn mean."

Madeline did not answer Sandra for a long time. She just shook her head knowingly, for she too had once felt the sting of Kim's spasmodic bursts of rac-ism.

Three week ago, when Kim had introduced Madeline to a new classmate, she had taken Madeline's arm and said to the new girl,

"This is my best V-i-e-t-n-a-m-e-s-e friend, Madeline. She's a nice chink! She's from South Vietnam.

The bad ones killing everybody on television are from North Vietnam."

Madeline remembered mumbling "Hi" to the new girl and then leaving the area abruptly before the girls could catch sight of the huge tears gently falling from her beautiful, delicately slanted eyes. Madeline was Vietnamese, and she was proud of it, but Madeline knew that Kim was not being complimentary. Why mention her background? What was the point? Kim seemed to be apologizing, with mockery, for the un-popular war raging in Vietnam and the fact that peo-ple of Madeline's heritage were connected to the vi-olence. Yes, Madeline knew how Sandra felt, and she moved a little closer to her friend. The two silently shared the burden of the oppressed as they traveled around the strip.

The music stopped! Sandra and Madeline head-ed back to the sideline, but they were unusually qui-et. Sandra saw Peter scoot over to Kim's chair. She watched as Kim pointed to her, and Peter shook his head, "No!" three times. A lump came into her throat, for she and Peter had been friends for such a long, long time. Skating doubles did indeed separate the

Black girls from the White girls. Sandra had thought that color made no difference, no more so than a girl wearing a blue jumper versus a girl wearing a red jumper. Who would choose someone over someone else just because they were wearing a blue jumper? Now she knew who would, and the pain returned.

Sandra and Madeline sat down a few seats away from Kim and Peter. The two girls were unusually quiet as they watched Peter and Kim chatter away. The recovery signs from two rounds of skating—deep breathing—were the only sounds between them.

This intermission was much, much longer than the first had been. The youngsters were well rested by the time Sister Catherine announced that it was time for the first sweetheart round.

"Boys and girls should pair up," she said, smiling.

Sandra and Madeline sat very still, waiting for a partner. Finally, Paul rolled over to Madeline and asked if she would skate with him. She stood up, and the two of them skated over to the strip, where Kim and Peter rolled by holding hands. Sandra remained behind. Sitting all alone. Nobody had asked Sandra to skate with them, and six boys had said they wanted to. In a room full of people, loneliness and solitude began to surround Sandra. The whole world was rejecting her. Before today, she had never noticed that they were all wearing blue jumpers- even the boys, even Madeline.

This was more than a little nine-year-old girl could take in one afternoon. The tears began to rise from deep inside of Sandra. She tried to blink them away, but they kept coming, and quietly they poured over her soft brown face. Her head felt heavy, and it was so hard to breathe. Being rejected hurts, and it hurts so much more when it comes from people you love. Oh God, it hurt so much!

Miss Sweeting, the teacher, glanced pityingly across the room at Sandra. She knew why Sandra was sitting alone as the others skated. But what could she do? Sandra was suffering from the tail end of an age-old pain. It was one that every Black who'd ever lived in this country, where all men were supposed to have been created equal, had been afflicted with at one time or another. Every decade seemed to suffer a little less than the one before, but that didn't make it any easier now for Sandra, the sufferer.

The room had become a blur to her. The kids were strangers. She had given them her heart, and they had stabbed her in the back.

"I hate white people," Sandra thought. "But I can't hate people," she remembered. "Hating is wrong! Well, so is not skating with your friend because her skin is black," she argued with herself.

Sandra was so confused. Nine years old and she had already learned that love could be painful.

Sandra stood up to leave. She wanted to go home, where people loved her. As she walked toward the telephone to call her dad, the music stopped, and Madeline glided over to her.

"Please don't leave, Sandra," Madeline pleaded.

"I know how you feel, but please stay. I'm your friend. I love you."

Sandra looked at Madeline. She knew that Madeline's affection was genuine. Not only was Madeline the smartest student in their fourth grade class, but she was also one of the nicest and most sincere girls in the whole school. She and Sandra spent a lot of time together -- playing, talking or studying-- and Sandra, not wanting to disappoint her friend, said,

"Okay, Maddy, I'll stay till the next sweetheart round, and then I'm going home."

The girls skated back to the chairs and sat down. Paul came over and brought Madeline a drink. Sandra watched as Peter brought a drink to Kim. No one brought a drink to Sandra.

The fourth round of skating came and went. By the fifth round Kim had rejoined Madeline and Sandra. The girls were skating together, but they were no longer holding hands.

Returning to the sidelines, Sandra looked up at the pretty balloons and streamers. It was then, for the first time that day, she noticed the crucifix. "What a joke!" Sandra thought. "If the Holy Spirit worked in people like they say it does, people wouldn't hurt other people so badly. The Holy Spirit is God. God is good. If this good God is inside of people, why do people act so mean?" Then a terrifying thought came over her, "What if God was White! He wouldn't skate with a Black girl either."

Sandra trembled! Her little body shook as the room darkened. Sandra's soul was lost. Would God reject her? Life without God was no life at all. Her faith-filled body quivered at the thought of ever being separated from God. Without hesitation, she turned to the crucifix and cried out, "God help me. I'm so afraid. Please help me. Please, please help me."

Sandra loved God with all her heart. Never was there a time that God was not with her. He was at Mass every week. He was at home every day. And He was in the Steverson living room when the family said the Rosary. He was in school. He was on the playground. He was at the store. He came to the movies. He was everywhere! Would God reject her too?

No! No! No!

God heard His child's fright-filled prayer. And Heaven, Itself, paused!

Instantly, Sandra felt a warm, gentle breeze engulf her fragile body.. The breeze was followed by angels, choirs of angels, all singing and whispering,

"God loves you Sandra! God loves you Sandra! God loves you Sandra!"

Immediately, the childish thought of ever being rejected by God passed from her mind almost as quickly as it had appeared for Sandra remembered that Sister Catherine had said, "God has no color. He loves everyone- black and yellow, red and white."

God loved her! God would skate with her! And if God loved her, she was still loveable!

Sandra's spirit soared, and her feet lightened. Sandra's innocence was skating away, but her hope lingered.

The music slowed down, but before Sandra could leave the skating rink, Christopher, one of the six, tapped her on the shoulder and said,

"Sandra, you promised that you would skate a round with me. Do you remember? Can we skate this round together?"

Sandra glowed. The whole world hadn't rejected her, only two people.

"I didn't forget, Chris," she said. "I'd like to skate this round with you."

Christopher beamed. He had wanted to skate the first sweetheart round with her, but yesterday when he'd asked her, she had told him that she had promised that one to Peter. He'd never even noticed that she had sat that round out alone. The two friends conversed for a moment, and then Christopher skated off to get Sandra a drink. Sandra rejoined Kim and Madeline on the sideline. When Christopher approached a minute later with Sandra's drink, Madeline smiled, and, looking a little surprised, Kim smiled also.

Sandra had just finished her drink when the music started up again. She set the paper cup down on the chair as Christopher extended his hand to her. Chattering away warmly, the pair headed for the strip.

"Times are certainly changing," Sister Catherine said to Miss Sweeting as they watched Sandra and Christopher move gracefully around the rink.

"They sure are!" Miss Sweeting responded lovingly, "God knows it's about time!"

Christopher smiled at Sandra as the couple waltzed along the strip. Sandra smiled back.

"Do your parents ever make mistakes?" Sandra asked her friend.

"Sure!" Christopher said. "Lots of them."

Sandra looked up once more at the crucifix, which by now seemed to have moved closer to her and Christopher. In fact, the shadow of it was touching every part of the strip. It was skating right along beside the youngsters.

"So do mine!" Sandra replied. "So do mine!"